# Stepwise

## *A Parent–Child Guide to Family Mergers*

James Dale
and
Alex Beth Schapiro

**Andrews McMeel
Publishing**

Kansas City

01 02 03 04 05 BIN 10 9 8 7 6 5 4 3 2 1

Library of Congress Cataloging-in-Publication Data

Dale, Jim, 1948–
    StepWise : a parent-child guide to family mergers / James Dale
and Alex Beth Schapiro.
        p. cm.
    ISBN 0-7407-1111-3 (pbk.)
    1. Stepparents. 2. Stepfamilies. 3. Parent and child. I. Title: Parent-
child guide to family mergers. II. Schapiro, Alex Beth. III. Title.

HQ759.92  .D345  2001
306.874—dc21
                                                        2001020207

Book design and composition by Kelly & Company

---

**ATTENTION: SCHOOLS AND BUSINESSES**

Andrews McMeel books are available at quantity discounts with bulk purchase
for educational, business, or sales promotional use. For information, please write
to: Special Sales Department, Andrews McMeel Publishing, 4520 Main Street,
Kansas City, Missouri 64111.

*Here's to all those stepkids out there.*
*I've got you covered.*

—Alex Beth Schapiro


*To my wife, Ellen,*
*who not only gave me her love,*
*but the chance to love her children.*

—Jim Dale

# Acknowledgments

Thanks to all the wise people who have made me a wise girl (from Socrates to the Dalai Lama to my mother). Oh yeah, and thanks to Jim, a man of a thousand dances whom I love dearly.

—Alex Beth Schapiro

Thanks to our editors, Allan Stark and Kelly Gilbert; our agent, David Black; and the people who helped make me a better parent and stepparent, Andy, Sara, and Alex.

—Jim Dale

# Introduction

Stepparenting is like coming into a movie after it's already started, trying to figure out what's going on, who's doing what to whom, and what's going to happen next, without asking everyone around you a lot of stupid questions.

This is a book about stepparenting written by a stepfather and stepdaughter who actually get along—most of the time. One of us has raised three children, two step- and one non-, two girls and one boy, from early teenage, preteen, and birth, respectively. The other has been a daughter and stepdaughter, sister and stepsister. As a family, we have three last names. We're veterans, if not experts.

This is about what we've each learned the past few years: There is a difference between *90210* and *Road Rules*. To a teenage girl, the phrase "white T-shirt" is the description of one of 104 different fashion items. Adults are anal (especially stepadults.) Homework is a multi-media experience, best done while e-mailing, watching television, wearing a Walkman, and talking on a cordless phone. Thunder is scarier when your mother isn't home. Grown-ups ask too many questions (especially step-grown-ups.) You can be adored, scoffed at, and have your shoulder cried upon, all in the same day. Stepparents (in fact, all parents) should just "chill."

What we have to offer is mostly common sense; but then again, common sense isn't very common. This is what has worked for us. We won't claim to know the final results for at least another decade. But so far, so good.

# StepWise

# 1

Wait.

As a stepparent, you want a close, warm, sharing, caring, deep relationship with your stepchildren immediately. They're not in as much of a hurry. You know you're a really swell person, but they're skeptical. After all, you have two strikes against you: You're new and you're a parent. (Just what every kid wants—an extra parent.)

Don't hurry the relationship. *Wait.* They'll let you know when they're going to let you into their lives. *Wait.* When they do let you in, they'll let you in slowly. *Wait.* Then wait some more. But when they finally decide that maybe you're okay, be ready . . . 24/7 . . . to be immediately close, warm, sharing, caring, and deep. In the meantime . . . *wait.*

# 2

---

## Adjust (lower)
## your expectations.

To all stepparents: Forget about being perfect. That halo you wore back when you were dating (*he's so funny*; *she brings us presents*) blows a fuse the day you get married (*his jokes are corny*; *what happened to the presents?*). Now you're just another adult who gets annoyed with them when they leave old Fruit Roll-Ups in their beds. Instead of perfect, aim for "not bad." This is, after all, parenting, where each generation's goal is just to screw up our children less than our parents screwed us up.

# 3

## Accept reality.

The kids already have a father or mother. In their game of life, he or she was the starter. You're the reliever. Step in. Throw your best stuff. But don't try to replace him or her on the roster. Don't compete. Don't second-guess. Don't criticize . . . even if your stepchildren do. (This can be difficult. Especially when Dad "forgets" it was his weekend and runs off to Vail with his massage therapist.)

Just be your solid, reliable, steady, understanding self. Kids are smart. Eventually they'll realize the role you play in their lives. (If they don't, you can always hire an out-of-work actor to stop by and say things like "That stepparent of yours sure is solid, reliable, steady, and understanding.") You may never be the real dad or mom. But you can be someone the kids count on.

# 4

---

## Study.
## There will be a test.

Take the time to learn the important stuff about your stepchildren. Birth dates; grades; classes; teachers (best and worst); names of friends (real and imaginary), dogs, cats, goldfish, gerbils; favorite colors, songs, TV shows, foods, shoes, sticky desserts; number of years/months/hours until they get driver's license; teams played on and position played; what's cool and what's gross (subject to constant change).

How do you learn all this stuff? Subtly. Don't quiz. Don't grill. Observe. Listen. Eavesdrop. Spy (see, you can make this kind of fun). Ask indirect questions. Like "Would you please pass the carrots and tell me the name of the coolest rap singer you know?"

Write it all down. Memorize it. Quiz yourself. These are not insignificant details. These are the defining facts of a child's life. (Like your golf handicap.) Knowing the details shows the kids that they matter to you. There's nothing more insensitive than referring to a goldfish by a gerbil's name. And speaking of names, it's also a good idea to learn your stepchildren's names. "Hey, you, the tall one!" is not a great bonding technique.

# 5

## Show up.

Go to your stepchildren's plays, pageants, try-outs, games, play-offs, matches, marches, walks, runs, marathons, decathlons, sing-a-thons, tap-a-thons, drum-a-thons, previews, revues, and déjà vus. Showing up shows the kids that their lives are part of your life. It shows that you care. It shows that you can stay awake through a whole midget ballet.

# 6

## Listen. Don't talk.

When your stepchild finally opens up and starts talking to you, resist the temptation to talk back. Just shut up. Pay attention. Let her or him know you're interested but DO NOT SPEAK. Anything beyond a muffled "hmm" should carry a stiff fine. Let her talk until she runs out of gas. You'll learn: what (or whom) she likes, doesn't like, is thinking, wants to know about, is annoyed with, can't figure out. She'll get comfortable, and the more comfortable she is, the more she'll talk.

But if you try to make actual two-way conversation, you risk giving her a moment to realize what is actually happening—that she's opening up to you. She'll stop in midword. The moment will be gone. And as with a sighting of the Loch Ness monster, you will have no real proof it ever happened.

So stick to the DO NOT SPEAK rule. Give positive feedback, such as eye contact, the occasional head nod, the thoughtful brow furrow, or, if you're feeling really gutsy, the "uh-huh, go on" facial contortion that's like asking a question but involves no words. *But let her do the actual talking.* If she does it once, eventually she'll do it again. Of course, it could take a while, which brings us back to the first rule of stepparenting: *Wait.*

# 7

## Learn Kidspeak.

When conversation finally breaks out, you may think you and your stepchild both speak English. Wrong. You speak adult and he or she speaks kid. Your vocabulary is comprised of twenty to twenty-five thousand words. His is made up of twelve words, tops. He isn't going to suddenly want to talk like a middle-aged accountant, uptight real estate lawyer, anal insurance adjuster, weekend golf junkie, geeky fly fisherman, or whatever you are. So you might as well become fluent in his language.

First, eliminate words with multiple syllables. Like *eliminate, multiple,* and *syllable.* Next, sprinkle the word *like* on sentences as you would salt on an ear of corn. In like no time, like you'll talk like kids and like they'll like like you. Later, alternate *you know* with *like.* To become totally fluent, learn Mumble-ese, the dialect of unfinished words. "I wen' over ta Jasonz howz an' we jes' like lizend ta ceedees till ya know. Wajudo?" "Juz like hung roun 'n' slep."* There! You're communicating with your stepchild.

Or, for an intense course in Kidspeak, watch the movie *Clueless* until you've memorized it.

---

*Caution: Do not try this language at work.

# 8

---

## Avoid the "step" word.

It carries negative connotations. As in Cinderella's evil stepmother. And don't try corny euphemisms like "other dad" or "extra mom" or "bonus parent." Kids have built-in b.s. detectors.

Instead of using *step*-titles, just refer to each other by your first names, like regular people do. When a grown man introduces an eight-year-old, the world can pretty much figure out who's who. (*This is Andrew. He's either my wife's son or a midget drinking buddy of mine.)* Same goes for the kids introducing you. *(This is Bob. You can probably tell by his ugly golf shirt and bald spot that he's not in my sixth-grade homeroom.)*

Think about it. Instead of being categories, you're being people. Who knows, one day one of the kids might accidentally refer to you as "Mom" or "Dad." You can nod nonchalantly and then later weep tears of joy in private.

# 9

---

## Eat pizza.

In America, millions of children are born addicted to pizza. They can eat pizza ad nauseum, so to speak. Their idea of variety is ordering pizza from different pizza places. Pizza Shack, Pizza Hovel, Pizza Condo, Pizza on Wheels, Pizza King, Pizza Pope, World o' Pizza, 1-800-PIZZA, Pizzas in Space, Pizza.com.

But it's not enough for the stepparent to just leave the pizza money on the kitchen counter.

A real stepparent eats pizza with the kids. No plates. No utensils. Right out of the grease-stained box, shoveled on your bare hand, oozing oil, point first, into your gaping mouth!

You and your stepchild are now one. You have shared the pie of life. Pizza is more than a food. It's a bonding agent, not just symbolically but scientifically. (Like plastic garbage bags, pizza cheese never decomposes in nature.) Once you and your stepchild eat pizza together, don't be surprised if communication improves. He or she might laugh at your jokes. Or tell you what happened in school. Or even ask your opinion. Why? Is it something in the pizza? No, you're breaking down major barriers. You've sat at the same table (or floor). You've shared their culture. You've found common ground (or floor). And admit it, greasy pizza is pretty good.

# 10

## Accept your new culture.

The family you're joining is like a country. You're an immigrant. Immerse yourself in their culture. Study it. Embrace their traditions, customs, and rituals. Assimilate.

They carry out Chinese food (no garlic, medium spicy, white-meat chicken, no water chestnuts, extra hoisin sauce) on winter Sundays but not summer Sundays. They adjust the thermostat in fifteen-degree increments and wonder how it suddenly got so hot or cold. Their unspoken rule is, it's okay to take all birthday presents back to the store just in case there's something better. They don't sit in the first fifteen rows at the movies. They don't sit in the last row on airplanes. Watching the news on TV in the morning is fine but not at night because it's too depressing to go to bed with bad news. They use a lot of toilet paper. They wave to the mailman for good luck. They use toothpicks at restaurants, but not at home.

In no time, you will be able to pass for one of them. Of course, like all immigrants, you worry that you'll be giving up your own traditions. But the opposite happens. Little by little, your customs will also be adopted by the rest of the family. They'll develop cravings for Swedish Fish and Twizzlers. The dishwasher will be loaded in the "right" order: cups, then glasses, then small bowls, then salad plates, then dinner plates, then large platters, then silverware, and, last, odd-shaped items. Instant coffee for one or two people, brewed coffee for three or more. Messes can build up on weekdays; cleaning frenzy every Friday. And everyone will want to use your electric pepper mill.

You will have achieved the American dream: the great melting pot, all in one family.

# 11

Take your stepchildren to
see movies you don't like.

For girls, anything really sappy or based on a
Brontë novel. For boys, anything where stuff
gets blown up. And for little kids, any morality
battle between good and bad cartoon animals
with the voices of famous actors (i.e., Jack Nich-
olson as the ravenous python and Meryl Streep
as the queen of the monarch butterflies).

Don't be surprised if you weep your way through two boxes of tissues in the sappy movies, feel adrenaline bursting out of your veins during the explosion scenes, and cheer out loud, along with a hundred seven-year-olds, when the good animals ultimately triumph (and they always do) over the bad ones.

# 12

Watch TV shows with
your stepchildren that
you'd never watch yourself.

You'll be subjected to three kinds of TV fare:
1) shows about groups of kids who live, rent-
free, in an oceanfront villa but don't have jobs
and sit around all day, talking about who went
out with who, who's gay, who's not, if they should
get jobs (no!), and how much everything "sucks";

2) afternoon talk shows about mother-daughter strippers, grade school principals who've had sex-change operations, and affairs between pets and their owners; and 3) warp-speed channel surfing of all one-hundred cable stations: "Seen it—seen it—don't wanna see it—Sara saw it—news, no way—weather, no way—seen it—cool—seen it—hated it—whoa! Tom Green, cool, seen it—seen it—nothin' on . . ."

Now, you may ask, why subject yourself to this audio-video torture? Because you're spending quality time with your stepchildren. Not high-quality time. Not even medium-quality time. Low-quality time. The lowest. Staring-straight-ahead time. Occasionally grunting time. Slack-jawed, blank-mind time. Your bodies are literally vegetating in butt-shaped couch nests. Your brains are deteriorating minute by commercial minute. But you and your stepchildren are doing it together. What better proof that you care about them? No Hallmark card could say as much.

*Warning:* You may find yourself sneaking out of work early to catch those afternoon talk shows (you wouldn't want to miss Obese Lovers Week), getting an uncontrollable urge to live rent-free in an oceanfront villa and talk about who "sucks," and developing channel surfer's thumb.

# 13

## Listen to their music.

This will be painful. It means letting the kids pick the radio stations in the car. Not golden oldies ("Kids, this is classic rock and roll"). Not public radio ("Hey, listen to this funny anecdote about a man who raises hens in Rhode Island"). Not sports ("Wait! Don't change stations! He's pitching a perfect game . . .").

No, you have to listen to their favorites: K-UTE—all Britney, all the time. W-KIL—

greatest rap stars in and out of prison. W-*%#!!—the sound of heavy metal, hard drugs, and unprotected sex.

Will you ever learn to like their music? No. Never. Not if you live to be a thousand years old. Though you might develop partial deafness, which would be a blessing. Will subjecting yourself to this sensory bombardment make your stepchildren think you're cool? Not a chance. But they may think you're slightly less uncool. Take progress in small doses.

# 14

## Communicate with your stepchildren.

Ask them to tell you about their day. This can be really interesting.

Then, when it's your turn, tell them about your day. Make up something. Your real day is way too dull.

# 15

---

## Share hobbies
## with your stepkids.

Let's say you fly-fish. No, forget that one. Kids
won't stand in cold water and be silent all day.
Let's say you do needlepoint. No, forget that one.
Too slow, dull, repetitious, and tedious. Let's
say you collect stamps. Too boring. Antique
collecting: Who wants old stuff? Read novels:
Too much like homework. Gardening: You get

dirty and might have to touch worms. Hmm . . . maybe you need different hobbies.

Okay, say you like to binge on Cheez Doodles, Mountain Dew, and brownies, veg out in front of the TV, and then sleep in your clothes until noon the next day. That's a hobby you can share with your stepchildren.

# 16

---

## Show an interest
## in their schoolwork.

What classes is he taking? Does she have a big
test coming up? What's his favorite subject? All
right, after gym, what's his second favorite?
How does she like her teachers? When's the
term paper due?

Okay, that's enough. It is, after all, schoolwork.

# 17

---

## Try good-natured kidding.

Teasing banter is often a way to break down barriers in any social setting. Jokes about funny-looking clothing, bizarre taste in music, or quirky personal habits are little ways to bring you and your stepchildren together . . . as long as you are the tea*see* and they are the tea*sers*. "We tape-recorded your snoring and put it on the telephone answering machine." "Did you go to your big meeting with that piece of lettuce in your teeth?" "We signed you up for the Psychic Shopping Channel." "Did you know that all your favorite songs are played in elevators?" "Nice sweater. Are those real bells knitted onto the snowman's hat?"

Smile. Laugh with them. Laugh at yourself.

But do not ever try trading barbs with the kids. They'll either a) think you're not funny or b) say you're an insensitive grown-up picking on a helpless child and have you turned in to Child Services and taken to jail (which they will later find to be a hilarious joke on you).

# 18

Get to know your
stepchildren's friends.

Be open, honest, and direct with your stepchildren and eventually you will gain their love
and trust.

If that doesn't work, cheat. Infiltrate their
ranks. Get a double agent. Win over one of
their friends.

It isn't easy, but if, somehow, you can actually
win over one of their friends, you'll have a secret

weapon more powerful than mind control.

How do you do it? The old-fashioned way: bribery. (Hey, think of it like the Olympics. Steroids may be wrong, but you know they'll be used.)

Good bribes include: new AA batteries for a Walkman. Gummi anything. A hot CD by a disgusting performer. A totally noneducational video game. A ride anywhere.

The fact that you a) provided them with something they needed and b) did not criticize them (as parents do) will make them like you, or at least think that maybe you're not a total loser. The friend will then pass this semipositive information on to your stepchild and have more credibility than you would ever have.

# 19

---

## You cannot buy your stepchildren's affections.

But you can rent them. Go to the mall and eat at the food court; shop at the Gap or Wet Seal or the Pierced Nun; get them tickets to a rock concert; drive them to and from but don't go into the rock concert; play Super Nintendo and lose (no problem because adult eye-hand coordination is twenty-six times slower than that of any child); buy them the complete boxed set of seasons one to five of *Real World*.

Or you can give in to what they truly want/need/covet more than life itself . . . a trip to Disney World or Disneyland. (The Disney people studied the DNA of children, especially step-children, and built their parks based on these genetic maps.) The kids will like you the whole time you're there, plus a few days before and after.

The point of these activities isn't really to spend a lot of money (despite the cost of mouse ears and an all-park pass). It's spending time doing what they want, not what you want them to want.

# 20

Try not to disagree with
your stepchildren . . .
especially on things that
don't matter much
(and only five things
really matter).

There is no percentage in disagreeing. Children
expect you to disagree with them. That's what

parents do. Particularly stepparents. They expect you to disapprove of: their compost heap of a bedroom; their using a small reservoir's worth of hot water each morning; sticky fingerprints on all doors, handles, phones, and TVs; broken toys left jagged side up behind the tires of your car; T-shirt messages promoting unnatural acts; demented rock-band posters; all-sugar diets; Popsicles left under blankets to melt; and endless visits from their ex-convict friends. They expect your disgust, dislike, distaste, intolerance, objection, and revulsion. In fact, you're constantly being tested on the Are-You-Going-to-Do-What's-Expected? Test.

So don't do what's expected. When your stepdaughter declares, "There's nothing more beautiful than a large facial tattoo," resist the temptation to say, "I think it's a sign of mental illness." That's what she expects you to say. To pass the test, nod. Or shrug. Or smile. She doesn't really want a scale model of a Harley-Davidson etched into her left cheek. It's just another one of those things that don't really matter.

*Okay, what are the five things that really do matter?* School, driving, alcohol, drugs, and sex. Face it. Everything else is just details. Save your disagreeing for the Big Five. And don't defend your view. Just invoke the Adult Rule ("Because I said so").

# 21

Try hard to agree with
them, especially on
things that don't matter
(and remember, only
five things really matter).

Agreeing is even harder than not disagreeing.
This means pretending that something you're
against is actually okay with you, something you

hate is something you like, wrong is right, bad is good. This is called lying. But it's for a worthy cause—family harmony. It requires stifling your deepest feelings, beliefs, and morals and twisting them into blatant falsehoods.

For example, if your stepson says, "When people get old and start complaining all the time, the government should just nuke 'em to make room for more kids," find a way to agree, such as, "I, too, think that we can find creative ways to use nuclear power."

And if, by some miracle, you discover that you can agree on any of the Big Five, seize the chance. *Your stepdaughter thinks mind-altering drugs aren't too good an idea. What a coincidence. So do you. Your stepson thinks driving a car without a seat belt while speeding, changing lanes, and switching radio stations might be a bit dangerous. Another coincidence. So do you.* Document your agreement. Have it notarized, sealed in an air-tight display case, and hung at the Smithsonian Institution.

# 22

---

## Compromise.

This is another word for "give in." You're the adult. You don't really want the last piece of birthday cake . . . even if it is your birthday. You don't really have to watch the last game of the World Series when a rerun of *Saved by the Bell* is on. There'll be another World Series next year, but this episode won't be played again for a couple of weeks.

Let your stepdaughter use the last of the

hot water to rinse the creme-gel-holding-body-lightener-detangler from her hair so she looks her best when she goes to field hockey practice. After all, you don't really need to take a shower before your big meeting to win the big account and get the big promotion and change the rest of your life.

Say you only have twenty dollars. You need gas for your car to get to work (see "big meeting" above.) Your stepson wants to eat lunch at the mall. Get your priorities in order and give him the twenty dollars. That red warning light on the gas gauge is just there to scare you: You can probably make it to the office. And even if you run out, some nice serial killer will stop on the highway and give you a ride. The kids will remember you as the stepparent who was willing to compromise and give in.

Okay, these may be exaggerated examples,

but the point is that you give and they get; the point is that they come ahead of you. (You may wonder, If you give in all the time, when will your kids learn to compromise? When they have kids.)

# 23

---

Deal with kids' fights
with the wisdom of Plato,
Henry Kissinger, Solomon,
Gandhi, and the Dalai Lama.

Any parent can yell or send kids to their rooms.
As the stepparent, you may be held to a higher
(and impossible) standard. You're asked to be
"fair," something that doesn't exist.

No matter who does what to whom and with what blunt instrument, you're not supposed to holler, threaten, lose your temper, ground, punish, grit your teeth, or even frown severely.

Like Plato, you weigh all sides of the skirmish. *He wanted to watch ESPN classic soccer reruns. She wanted to watch* Fashion Emergency. Like Kissinger, you consider the reactions of both parties. *She licked his sandwich. He put her Beanie Baby in the Cuisinart.* Then, like Solomon, you find a solution so brilliant that both sides see its wisdom. *We will divide the television in two, so each of you gets half but neither can watch it.* When one of the kids goes for the chain saw, it's time for Gandhi. *I will sit in the corner and starve until you two work out your differences.*

After two weeks of starving, get up, go to your own room, and scream. That's what the Dalai Lama does when the stress gets to him.

When your stepkids fight, don't expect to settle their battles any better or worse than a regular parent would.

# 24

---

## Wait for the calm after the storm.

Here's a practical suggestion for settling interkid problems: Don't do it right away. Whatever it is, let it cool. Come back to it later . . . in an hour or a day or a week. See if whatever it was that they were battling over still matters to either combatant. If it still does, come back even later . . . say, in another decade. Kids rarely stay mad at each other for more than seven years.

# 25

Never, ever, ever take
your stepchildren's side
against your spouse,
no matter how wrong
you think he or she was.
Never ever.

Taking the stepkids' side against their mother
or father may temporarily make points with the

kids, but it will result in you sleeping on the couch for the rest of your life. (And the kids will realize that you were just sucking up to them anyway.)

# 26

Don't get too
affectionate with
your husband or
wife in front of
the stepchildren.

It will make them puke. (This applies to all
children, not just step-.)

# 27

Don't let little foibles,
phobias, eccentricities,
or disgusting habits
get to you.

All kids do stuff that gets on your nerves. The
difference is, if they're your kids, there's at least
a 50 percent chance they inherited their habits
from you, so getting mad at them is like getting
mad at yourself. With stepchildren, there's a

100 percent chance they didn't inherit their habits from you, so you may not recognize and sympathize with the habits as easily.

Solution? Self-hypnosis. You are getting sleepy. Close your eyes. Close your ears. Give up all standards of normal behavior. When you wake up, it simply will not bother you that your step-children: chew with their mouths open; talk while chewing with their mouths open; burp while talking and chewing with their mouths open; never close the front door; never close the back door; never close the refrigerator door; never close the bathroom door; miss the toilet bowl; don't flush; feign deafness when things need to be done; have an irrational fear of insects, night noises, the dark, dentists, shampoo in their eyes, relatives' kisses, and long thin vegetables; don't have a rational fear of snakes; hate foods touching each other on their plates;

eat only meats with no visible fat; turn everything on and nothing off; cry out in pain when their shirt itches or their socks are tight; and lose the cordless phone at least once a week.

When you wake up, if self-hypnosis isn't working, go back to sleep.

# 28

---

## Develop filth blindness.

You have two choices when it comes to kids' dirt. You can attempt to be the first person in the history of the world to convince a child to suddenly become clean . . . or you can give up.

Now that you've decided to give up, here's how. Close your eyes (and nose) to the following: laundry mountains, bathtub terrariums, airborne tuna-sandwich viruses, sweat-sock stench, indoor mud, towel mildew, dog poop on shoe bottoms, backpack insect colonies, human-sized hair balls, pocket slime, fingernail gardens, scalp parasites, sneaker fungus, and sticky skin.

Close your eyes? Yes. Look right at filth and pretend it isn't there. Stare grime in the face and ignore it. Deny the reality of dirt. Step over it. Hold your nose. Wear gloves. Just reject the existence of dirt. Because you won't change the kids. But, believe it or not, they will clean up sometime between seventh grade and marriage, through no influence of yours.

Or you can try to convince them of the merits of emptying their book bag of last year's lunches . . . you clean freak!

# 29

Relax. Make mistakes.
Screw up. Commit
blunders, bloopers,
and bumbling errors.
(Okay, don't overdo it.)

No matter how hard you try to do everything
right, you're going to do things wrong. You're
going to make mistakes. Many, many mistakes.
You don't want to know how many.

Okay, here's how many. Figure five to seven on the typical weekday. Adding in triple figures for weekends, holidays, and vacations, that's sixty to seventy-five per week. Then the number temporarily doubles during the teenage years. So, on average, roughly five thousand official, capital "M" Mistakes, plus another one thousand to fifteen hundred misdemeanors, annually.

But hey, that's not bad. Not only will your screwups provide endless entertainment for your stepchildren, but whenever you're not committing a boneheaded move, you are, by absence of error, doing something right, or at least okay.

Relax. To err is human. You're just really human.

# 30

---

What if, no matter
how hard you try to be
perfect, you and your
stepchild f-i-g-h-t?

It's not a question of *whether* you and your stepchild are going to have a fight but what to
do *when* you have a fight. You can be reason-
able, even-tempered, unflappable, compromising,

enlightened, mature, wise, or just a wimpy, spine-less pushover, and you're *still* going to fight, someday, sometime, about something.

So when the inevitable happens, then what? How long will you let it last? How much will it escalate? Will it be yelling-ballistic or stewing-seething? How will you make peace?

First of all, realize that all fights (step- or non-) are the same. They're not about what they're about (the missing skateboard wheel, TV, who didn't return the green sweater, reading personal e-mail, or the message no one took). They're about somebody's feelings.

But . . . stepfighters' feelings are even more sensitive than nonstepfighters'. Think about that. Think how sensitive a regular parent or child, or both, can get. Square it. Cube it. Infinity it.

Because both stepparticipants are afraid of

the same thing. Not being treated as "real." As in, real parent, real child, or real member of the family. *Who does he think he is to tell me what to do? What makes her think I have to listen to what she says? Doesn't he have any respect for me? Doesn't she know how much I care about her? How could he hurt my feelings this way after all I've done?*

So the ways to settle stepfights are the same ways you settle all fights, only more so.

1. Treat each other as "real." (Show it, don't say it.) That means, let the fight happen. Don't turn yourself inside out with torture: *Oh my God, we had a fight, it's the end of the world!* It's the beginning of the "real" world. Then . . .

2. Let feelings cool. A little longer. Let everyone get over it, whatever it was. If that doesn't work . . .

3. Try to talk. Try harder. Slowly, non-threateningly, patiently, gently explore why you both got upset. If he or she isn't ready . . .

4. Talk about something else. Neutral. Really neutral. Sports scores, snack foods, rating the best toy stores, romance novels, Pokémon, school closings due to weather (anything but homework, room cleaning, or personal hygiene). Or . . .

5. Put yourself in his or her position. Not just for a split second but really. Is it possible you were wrong? This is a hard thing for adults to admit. (Even though adults insist that kids admit it.) If you were wrong, it's okay to say so.

6. Don't be a total wimp and say you were wrong if you know, in your heart, you weren't.

This never works with anyone. You'll resent it, and the child will see through it.

7. Declare peace. Sometimes a fight should just be over. Sometimes it lasts so long that neither person knows how to end it. Especially extrasensitive stepfighters. That's when one of you should just say it's over and move on. Or just move on. That's how most fights end anyway.

But wait! What about who was right and who was wrong? What about learning his or her lesson? What about respect? It's all there. It happened during the fight and the feud period. That's when all the important stuff sinks in. You'll f-i-g-h-t, but you'll get over it. Just treat each other as "real," only more so.

# 31

---

## Find time to
## spend one on one.

Kids like attention. Who doesn't? You certainly do. Stepkids may even want more because their lives have changed. One parent doesn't live there anymore. The result? Net loss of time spent with child. New person moves in with remaining parent. The result? Net loss of time spent by remaining parent with child. Bottom line: less attention paid to stepchild.

It isn't intentional, and it will all work out over time. But in the short run, it may not feel so good. Find reasons to spend time, one on one, with each of your stepchildren. Even if he or she acts like he or she couldn't care less about getting attention.

YOU: *You want to go to the hardware store with me?*

STEPDAUGHER: *If you want me to go, I'll go.*

She wants to go. Take her. Stop for frozen yogurt on the way back. It's the least you can do after she walked up and down the "bits, augers, and ratchets" aisle. Try a similar approach with your stepson.

YOU: *Who's that singer on TV?*

STEPSON: *A guy.*

YOU: *What guy?*

STEPSON: *A rapper.*

YOU: *Which one?*

STEPSON: *A mean one.*

YOU: *Oh, that one.*

*Long pause.*

STEPSON: *His name's Corpse Dog. I've got his CD. Wanna hear it?*

YOU: *Okay.*

It doesn't matter what you do with your step-kids, just do something. Not every minute or every day. Just let him or her know that you're there. You'll think of things to do. If you can't, read the next suggestion.

# 32

## Buy something major together.

Okay, this one is definitely going to cost you money. But there's nothing quite so bonding as making a big purchase. Big purchases are big decisions. Big decisions are usually made by big people. Which annoys the heck out of little people.

On the other hand, including your stepchild says a lot without saying it. It says you value his or her opinion. It says you're a family. It says you don't do things unilaterally, like a power-mad dictator. If the "thing" you're buying is technical, it says you're pretty much in a haze and need the help of someone who isn't gizmo-challenged. If it's the latest "thing," it says you admit that you're stuck in the past and need to be guided by your stepchild's hand of coolness. If the "thing" is a car, it says other people (i.e., stepchildren) will ride in it, maybe even drive it, and don't want to be seen in their parents' embarrassment-mobile. If the "thing" falls in the wide-screen TV/surround sound/DVD category, it's an admission that you don't know a) the difference between a wide screen and a skinny screen, b) what to do if you're ever surrounded by sound, c) what D,V, or D stands for and you want someone to go with you so the salesman doesn't pick on you. And if the "thing" just costs a whole lot, it says, Boy this thing costs a lot, I'm not making this decision alone!

Making a big purchase together will bring you together. Of course, "big" is a relative term. It can be anything from a motor home to a cordless phone, as long as it's a big deal at your house. The important thing is, buying it means time spent together. And time is more important than money. Though it costs money to get the time. Anyway, you get the idea.

# 33

Teach your stepchild
to parallel park.

If you really want to get close to a stepchild, take on a truly challenging job. But one that may be easier for you than for a "real" parent. Like parallel parking. (Nothing is more difficult to learn, including building your own microchip, than parallel parking.)

*Just pull alongside the car parked in the space ahead of the space you want. Not quite so far into the street. You have to park the car within walking distance of the curb. Try again. Okay, not so close to the other car. I can see my nostril hairs reflected in the car's paint job. Now back up slowly, turning the wheel so the car curves gently toward the curb. Not into the curb. Not over the curb. Not on the sidewalk. Not inside the dry cleaner's! Now pull forward just short of the next car's bumper. Okay, you didn't hit the bumper that hard. It was probably loose enough to fall off already. Now back up slowly. I guess the car behind you had a loose bumper too. There, you're in. Now pass me the bottle of Advil and rub my forehead.*

Chances are, compared to the actual parent, you won't get as angry, won't lose your temper as fast, won't rattle off a string of four-letter helpful hints when bumpers get bumped, fenders get bent, or trees get leveled. You'd lose your cool in a split second if it were your child, but it's that one-step removal that makes you a lot calmer. And makes the two of you closer. So what if it costs you a taillight or hood ornament, or side-view mirror, or garage wall, or the price of re-placing that lineup of minivans, luxury SUVs, and Bavarian sports cars that your stepdriver just sideswiped at fifty miles an hour. It's only money. A lot of money!! Take it easy. Remember, you're the calm stepparent.

# 34

---

## Show your dorky side.

This shouldn't be too difficult. You can just be yourself. If you're an adult, you are, by definition, dorky.

You dress dorky. Your pants probably ride on your waist instead of drooping around the lower third of your butt. Or your skirt is wider than a belt and looser than a tourniquet. Your shoes are tied. And you usually wear only one shirt at a time. Your music is dorky. What are you humming? Show tunes??!! Your car is dorky: It has four doors. Your worries are dorky: nutrition, sleep, regularity. You talk about stuff like the weather and forgetting someone's birthday. You have this obsession with things being clean, like dishes and floors. And you're a sap. You weep. You even save old junk from your past and you dig it out and make them look through it. Like baby bracelets, pressed prom flowers, that debate team runner-up award, and, of course, your old high school yearbook where you really look like a dork . . . even to you. Because why? Now you get it. You're a dork.

All of this is cause for endless entertainment, amusement, and reassurance to stepchildren. It shows that you're vulnerable. If you're vulnerable, they can afford to like you. They're vulnerable too.

# 35

---

## Ask them big
## life questions.

Kids don't want to talk to adults about important boring things, but they will talk about
important interesting things. Translation: They
don't want to talk about why they can't do their
homework *and* clean their room in the same
week, but they will talk about how they plan to
be secretary-general of the United Nations, a
rap/rock/movie star, and the environmental

scientist who patches up the hole in the ozone, simultaneously.

They don't want to talk about who forgot to feed the bird (and why now he's not moving) or how the TV remote control got into the refrigerator, but they will talk about how plants can have their feelings hurt, what if you slept for twenty years, food pills, moving things with your mind, X-ray vision, and what they'd wish for if they had one wish in the whole world.

They want to talk about the things they think about but no one ever asks them about. The really important things. Ask. You'll learn something.

# 36

Don't force your own children and your stepchildren together.

They'll irrationally but instantly hate each other and rationally but also instantly hate you for setting them up. They'll stare at each other silently. Then they'll stare at you silently afterward. After the silence, they'll mutter. You won't be able to make out their actual words, so instead you'll imagine they're saying horrible things about you, your children, themselves, their life, North America, the Western Hemisphere, and the twentieth and twenty-first centuries, and even though they're not really saying those things, you'll convince yourself they are, and feel awful and never forgive yourself.

But if you still think it's a good idea, by all means, get the whole brood together.

Or . . . let them discover each other on their own timetable. When? You'll know. Basically, later. When later comes, they'll get together willingly and easily, because by then they'll be used to you and their other "stepwhatevers." And they'll be able to agree with their step-siblings on at least one thing: what dorks their parents are. Pretty soon, they may even like each other, and they'll get together on their own to talk about what dorks their parents are. And you can stare at them silently.

# 37

---

## Don't compete with kids for attention.

This should be obvious . . . but it isn't. Stepkids don't want to think a new person joined the family and stole the spotlight. The kids are still the princes and princesses of the domain. You are, after all, an adult, so you should know not to compete for attention. But you're human, so you probably want some attention. Get it later.

When the kids are out, or you're out, or after they go to bed. In other words, grow up. Or at least act like a child only when the children aren't around.

# 38

## Don't be New Age.

It's tempting to be cool. To show the kids that their stepmother or stepfather isn't like every other mom or dad. *You're different.* But here are three suggestions: Don't. Don't. And don't.

Don't try to cure teenage acne with acupuncture. Don't have after-dinner incense burning and free-association poetry sessions. (Both stink.) No sitar music. No crystals. No kaftans. No berets. (In fact, no hats of any kind.) Unless you can swear, under oath, that you love the taste of tofu, don't make turkey-shaped tofu and call it Thanksgiving. Don't move the stereo and wide-screen TV around the house in the name of feng shui. (And don't ever move the satellite dish once it's lined up.) Don't ask the kids' friends to come over for hot chocolate and channeling dead relatives. Don't align planets, figure out whose house Mercury is in, or buy tanks of pure oxygen.

You see, kids don't want "different." They want "the same." The same as every other kid on earth. The last thing they want is a stepmom or stepdad who is different. They want one who is the same.

Don't be New Age. You're old age.

# 39

---

## Don't embarrass them.

This has been covered thoroughly earlier. But just in case, before you do anything, ever, of any kind, in front of anyone, ask yourself, "Is there any chance my stepchildren might be embarrassed by this?" When in doubt, do nothing. Say nothing. Ask nothing. Hum nothing. Don't smile. Don't frown. Don't chew. Don't breathe any more than necessary. Just sit motionless. There. You're not embarrassing your stepchildren. Now keep it up.

# 40

---

## Show them
## you care . . .
## in private.

Show your stepchildren your support. Let them
know you're there when and if they ever need
you. Tell them you love them. *But* . . . never do
this in front of anyone else. (See No. 39, "Don't
embarrass them.")

# 41

Create a history that
belongs to you and
your stepchildren.

No matter how short a time you've all been together, get nostalgic. Use expressions like "the
good old days," "fond memories," "remember
when . . .," and "how about the time . . .?" Take
pictures of everything. Mount the pictures in
albums. Make everyone sit around and look at

the pictures. Shoot videotape. Make the kids watch the videos after dinner. Give all shared adventures their own titles, such as: "The Casserole That Looked Like Vomit Story," "The Dog Ate My Tie Story," "The Kids Cried the First Time They Met Me Story." The sooner you can all look back on things, the longer it seems as if you've been part of one another's lives.

What's great is that every single thing you do is a potential memory. *Remember when we went to the mall . . . on Saturday? Remember when we cut the lawn . . . also on Saturday? Remember when we ate dinner . . . tonight?* And memories are something you and your stepchildren can have forever. *Remember when the electrical storm knocked out the power and we read ghost stories by flashlight? Remember when your mother and I locked you out of the bedroom for two hours?*

# 42

---

## Holiday traditions.

Every family has holiday traditions. In stepfamilies, the most common tradition is feeling happy and sad at the same time. That's when stepkids think about the parent they're with and the one they're not with. If they feel good, they feel bad for feeling good. If they feel bad, they just feel bad. And they can't help but think about *what if*: What if their parents had never split, what if everyone was still together, what if . . .?

So if there was ever a time for you, the step-parent, to be your best, this is it. Be sensitive. Be caring. Be part of your new family. Whatever their traditions are, be open to them. If they have a five-piece trading rule for Halloween candy, make out your protected list. If they open Christmas presents on Christmas Eve, declare Eve right after lunch. If they celebrate New Year's at 3:14 A.M. in honor of the year the clocks stopped, drink a lot of coffee and be prepared to stay up way past the ball falling. If they add an extra night to Hanukkah . . . well, you know what to do.

Join in. Add a few twists of your own (dress the dog like a Pilgrim.) Pretty soon, your new family will have its own old traditions.

# 43

---

## Don't try too hard. (Try hard to not try too hard.)

Yes, you want a great relationship. No, you can't force it. There's no such thing as a full-court press in child rearing. No prize for building a relationship fast.

Relax. Take it easy. Let things happen or not. Use the word *whatever*. Slouch. Shrug. Be yourself.

Unless you're an intense person. Then, by all means, be someone else. Someone cool, blasé, easygoing . . . but inside, bent on a mission to win over the stepchildren. Just don't show it.

# 44

---

## Stepchildren
## are not a species.

No matter how many hints, secrets, lessons, or rules you learn about raising stepchildren, remember, there is no such thing as "them." Each one is an individual. Recognize differences and treat each child differently. Equally, but differently. There is no "them," only him or her.

# 45

---

You win.

Most people get to have only one family. You get to have two. Sometimes it seems as if it's twice as hard. Mostly, it's twice as good (at least). More kids, more stories, more diapers, more fevers, more hugs, more nicknames, more homework, more spills, more cleanups, more birthdays, more cavities, more braces, more forgotten lunches, more romances and more breakups, more big games, big wins, and big losses, more dogs, cats, and gerbils, more stains on the carpet, more relatives, more trips, more photos in the albums, more laughing, more crying, more big moments and little moments, more memories, and more pizza. More is good.

# StepWise

## Developing Futures Inc.
3824 1a Street SW, Calgary, Alberta T2S 1R5

**Jane Warren**
403 660 2200
jane@developingfutures.com